Paris, China

François Prost

HOXTON MINI PRESS

Tianducheng, China

Photographer's note

I have always been fascinated by urban architecture. I remember the first time I went to Venice: I was 23 and travelled by train from Paris alone. When I emerged from the station, I had this strange feeling of not knowing whether my surroundings were real or not because I had seen them countless times in school books, magazines and films. I had the same sensation when I visited Rome and New York too. I learned later about Stendhal Syndrome – when humans find forms of art so beautiful it can make them ill – and how tourists visiting Paris or Florence for the first time had experienced this.

Some years later I read a few articles about architectural projects which explained that in China they were building replicas of typical European monuments such as Austrian villages, French châteaus, Venetian Renaissance buildings, Dutch towns, elements of Parisian architecture and more. I'd seen compelling miniatures of famous buildings from around the world in amusement parks, or in places like Las Vegas or Dubai. In this case, though, it seemed more extreme, more obsessive. The places in China were much bigger: entire mini neighbourhoods with people living there.

I began to research Tianducheng, an architectural development known as 'Sky City', located in a suburb of Hangzhou, east China. Tianducheng boasts an impressive 31km² of convincing Parisian architecture including its own Eiffel Tower (as seen on the previous spread). Scouring the internet, I tried to find as many examples that looked the same or similar to Parisian architecture. I did a test shoot in Paris, where I live, and decided there were enough elements to make a photo series. I found a cheap plane ticket to China in low season and booked the only room on Airbnb in the area. I lucked out on the weather but nobody I met could speak a word of English. With no access to Google, I had to use a translation dictionary to communicate with people, even with my Airbnb host. That was weird.

When I returned to Paris, I worked in reverse, travelling to different corners of the city, with the occasional trip to Versailles, to capture various façades, statues, fountains, artworks and so on. And so, my *Paris, China* diptychs were formed. I do hope the eerie similarities (and the differences) make you smile… but don't make you sick.

François Prost

François Prost

François is a Parisian photographer, graphic designer and art director. When he's not working for editorial or commercial clients he spends his time on personal photography projects, documenting façades of local French nightclubs, machine gun shops in the US and Chinese scooters. In 2020 he started photographing the similarities between the real Venice and replicas in Las Vegas and Hangzhou, China.

Hoxton Mini Press

Hoxton Mini Press is an indie publisher based in east London, started by Martin, a photographer, and Ann, who worked in galleries for many years. They are dedicated to making photography books more accessible (and playful) and think that as the world goes ever more online beautiful books should be cherished. They have two dogs, Moose and Bug, who don't give a crap about art but would like to visit Paris and China for gastronomic reasons.

France

Paris

China

Tianducheng

Paris, France

Tianducheng, China

Paris, France

Tianducheng, China

Paris, France

Tianducheng, China

Paris, France

Tianducheng, China

Paris, France

Tianducheng, China

Paris, France

Tianducheng, China

Paris, France

Tianducheng, China

Paris, France

Tianducheng, China

Versailles, France

Tianducheng, China

Versailles, France

Tianducheng, China

Paris, France

Tianducheng, China

Paris, France

Tianducheng, China

Versailles, France

Tianducheng, China

Versailles, France

Tianducheng, China

Versailles, France

Tianducheng, China

Versailles, France

Tianducheng, China

Paris, France

Tianducheng, China

Versailles, France

Tianducheng, China

Paris, France

Tianducheng, China

Paris, France

Tianducheng, China

Paris, France

Tianducheng, China

Paris, France

Tianducheng, China

Paris, France

Tianducheng, China

Paris, France

Tianducheng, China

Paris, France

Tianducheng, China

Paris, France

Tianducheng, China

Paris, France

Tianducheng, China

Paris, France

Tianducheng, China

Paris, France

Tianducheng, China

Versailles, France

Tianducheng, China

Paris, France

Tianducheng, China

Paris, France

Tianducheng, China

Paris, France

Tianducheng, China

Paris, France

Tianducheng, China

Paris, France

Tianducheng, China

Paris, France

Tianducheng, China

Paris, France

Tianducheng, China

Paris, France

Tianducheng, China

Paris, France

Tianducheng, China

Paris, France

Tianducheng, China

Paris, China
First edition

Copyright © Hoxton Mini Press, 2020
All rights reserved

Photography © François Prost
Design by Daniele Roa
Copy-editing by Faith McAllister
Production by Anna De Pascale

ISBN 978-1-910566-78-7

A CIP catalogue record for this book is available from the British Library

First published in the United Kingdom in 2020
by Hoxton Mini Press

Printed and bound by Ozgraf, Poland

www.hoxtonminipress.com

a gnès b.
endowment fund

This project is kindly supported by Agnès b. endowment fund